Light Rails

Quinn M. Arnold

seedlings

CREATIVE EDUCATION • CREATIVE PAPERBACKS

Published by Creative Education and Creative Paperbacks
P.O. Box 227, Mankato, Minnesota 56002
Creative Education and Creative Paperbacks
are imprints of The Creative Company
www.thecreativecompany.us

Design by Ellen Huber
Production by Angela Korte and Colin O'Dea
Art direction by Rita Marshall
Printed in the United States of America

Photographs by Alamy (Theodore Silvius, Wiskerke),
Dreamstime (Fallsview), Getty Images (DuKai photographer),
iStockphoto (arinahabich, BeyondImages, bjeayes,
brianbalster, Davel5957, Gannet77, MarinMtk, PomInOz,
versevend), Shutterstock (Tommy Alven, Leonid Andronov,
anweber, Salvador Aznar, e X p o s e)

Library of Congress Cataloging-in-Publication Data
Names: Arnold, Quinn M., author.
Title: Light rails / Quinn M. Arnold.
Series: Seedlings.
Includes bibliographical references and index.
Summary: A kindergarten-level introduction to light rails,
covering their drivers, role in transportation, and such
defining features as their pantographs.
ISBN 978-1-64026-240-9 (hardcover)
ISBN 978-1-62832-803-5 (pbk)
ISBN 978-1-64000-375-0 (eBook)

This title has been submitted for CIP processing under LCCN
2019938377.

CCSS: RI.K.1, 2, 3, 4, 5, 6, 7; RI.1.1,
2, 3, 4, 5, 6, 7; RF.K.1, 3; RF.1.1

First Edition HC 9 8 7 6 5 4 3 2 1
First Edition PBK 9 8 7 6 5 4 3 2 1

TABLE OF CONTENTS

Hello, light rails!

Light rails are passenger trains.

These small trains can go almost anywhere.

A light rail runs on metal tracks. The train has only a few cars. But it can carry many people.

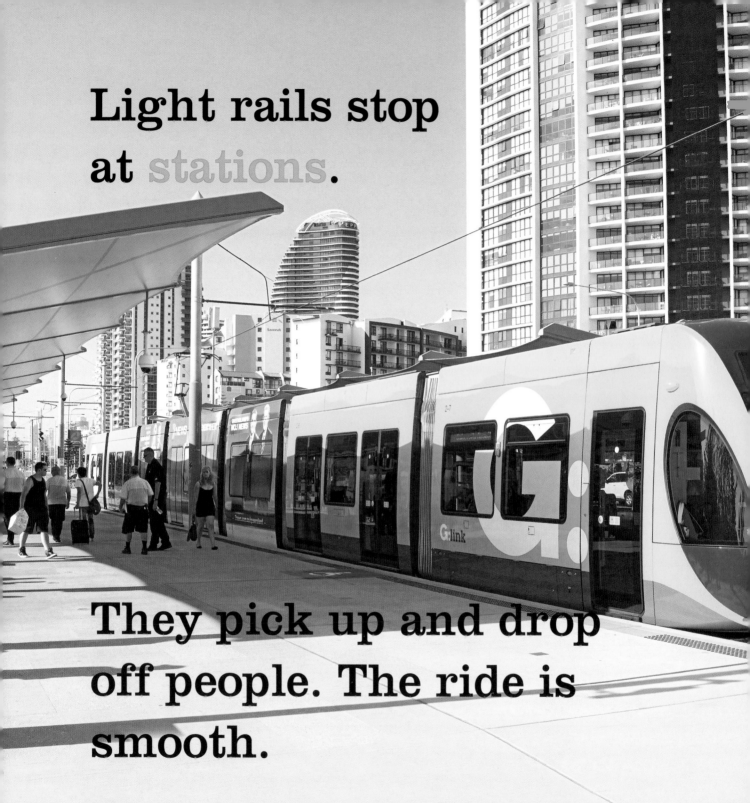

Light rails stop at stations.

They pick up and drop off people. The ride is smooth.

Passengers can sit or stand.

A light rail is powered by electricity. Power lines hang above the train. A pantograph runs along the lines.

An operator drives
a light rail.

Signal lights tell the operator when to stop or go.

Light rails go
through big cities.
They zoom along
busy streets.

Goodbye, light rails!

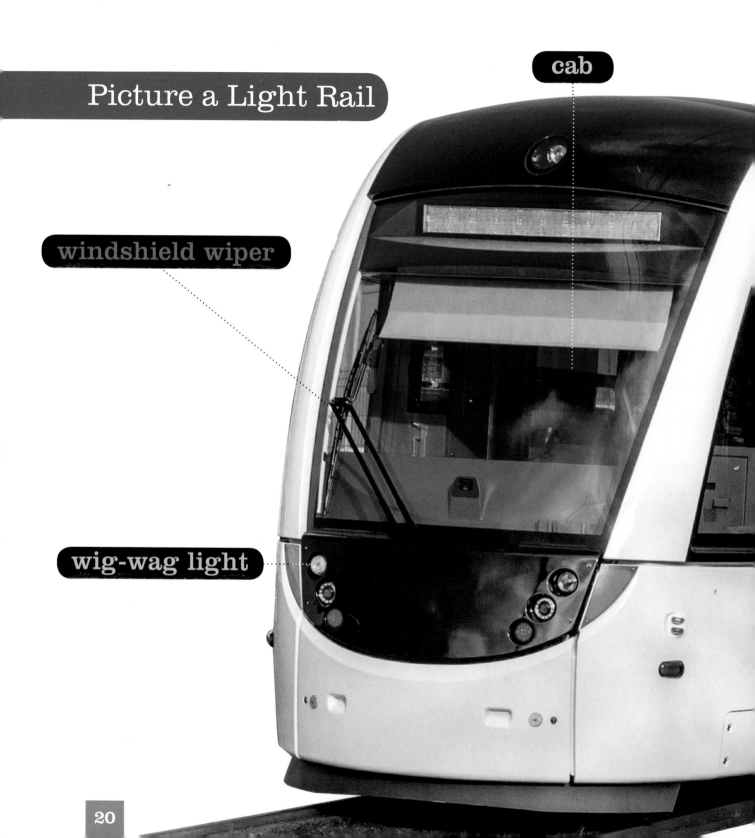

Picture a Light Rail

cab

windshield wiper

wig-wag light

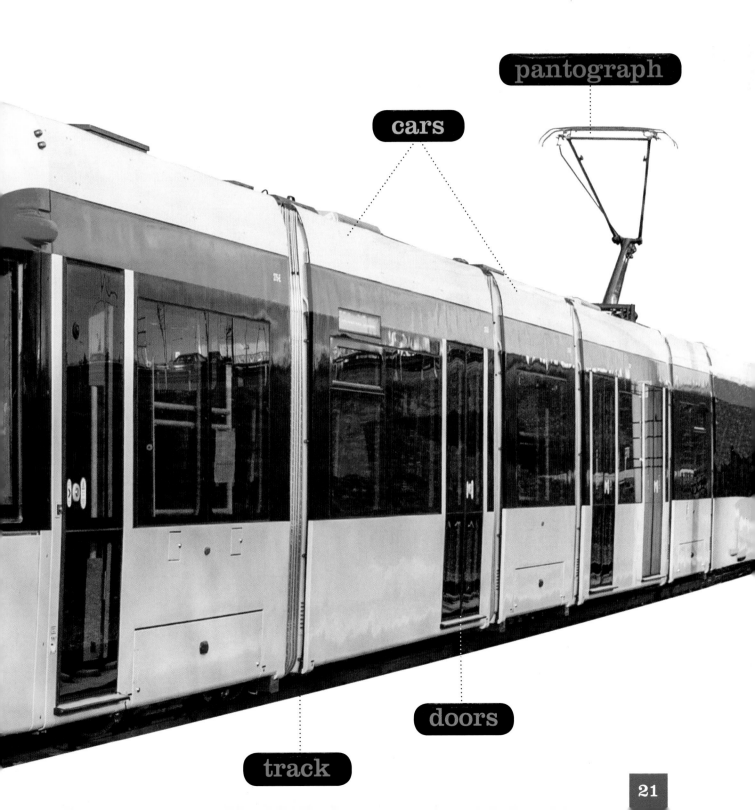

pantograph

cars

doors

track

21

Words to Know

cars: parts of trains where people sit or goods are carried

pantograph: the metal frame that carries electricity from overhead wires to a train

stations: the places where trains pick up and drop off people

Read More

Leighton, Christina. *City Trains*.
Minneapolis: Bellwether Media, 2018.

Williams, John Matthew. *Trains Go!*
New York: Gareth Stevens, 2018.

Websites

DK Find Out!: Electric Trains
https://www.dkfindout.com/us/transportation/history
-trains/electric-trains/
Learn more about trains powered by electricity!

Hello Kids: Train Coloring Pages
http://www.hellokids.com/r_711/coloring-pages
/transportation-coloring-pages/train-coloring-pages
Print out pictures of different kinds of trains to color.

Index